Are You Making Money for Your Hive?

Lessons in Getting Results through Learning

Karie Holton and Elwood Holton

OPEN BOOK
EDITIONS
A Berrett-Koehler Partner

ARE YOU MAKING MONEY FOR YOUR HIVE?
LESSONS IN GETTING RESULTS THROUGH LEARNING

iUniverse books may be ordered through booksellers or by contacting:

iUniverse
1663 Liberty Drive
Bloomington, IN 47403
www.iuniverse.com
1-800-Authors (1-800-288-4677)

Because of the dynamic nature of the Internet, any web addresses or links contained in this book may have changed since publication and may no longer be valid. The views expressed in this work are solely those of the author and do not necessarily reflect the views of the publisher, and the publisher hereby disclaims any responsibility for them.

Any people depicted in stock imagery provided by Thinkstock are models, and such images are being used for illustrative purposes only. Certain stock imagery © Thinkstock.

ISBN: 978-1-4917-3263-2 (sc)
ISBN: 978-1-4917-3264-9 (e)

Printed in the United States of America.

iUniverse rev. date: 4/11/2014

Introduction

Every day, millions of employees attend some type of training or learning event. Unfortunately, our best estimates are that only 10 to 30 percent of what they learn will ever be used in their work. In the United States alone, this means that around $250 *billion* is wasted every year.

Academics call this the "learning transfer problem." Put simply, *learning transfer* means that people use what they learn to do their jobs better, more efficiently, or differently. Poor learning transfer is the number one problem in employee development today. In our global knowledge economy, no organization can afford learning that does not result in improved performance. Yet little progress has been made toward solving this problem.

This fable is about two honeybees, Buzz and Buster. Buzz uses learning to produce lots of honey for his hive, and as a result, he and his hive mates enjoy a prosperous and productive life. Their hive is successful. Buster, on the other hand, looks around and sees lots of honey in his hive and so ignores the need to learn how to make more. Eventually, his hive runs out of honey, and nobody knows what to do. Thankfully, Buster finally learns from Buzz how to collect nectar from flowers to make honey and does the hard work necessary to save his hive.

We wrote this fable to teach everyone how important learning transfer is to organizations. CEOs should care about this problem, because they are wasting valuable resources every day. Human resources directors should care, because they are usually the ones charged with getting results from learning. Trainers should care, because without results, learning is useless to the organization.

The point of this story is that *everyone* should care about the problem. It's not just a management problem, and it's not just an HR problem. It's a problem that affects every person in an organization. Like Buster, many employees think they can ignore what they learn and keep doing things the way they always have. The result is that the organization eventually gets into trouble because there is no more "honey." When that happens, everyone suffers.

In today's organizations, all employees must constantly learn *and* use what they learn to improve their performance. The global economy is simply too competitive to rely on old ways of doing things. Workers like Buzz who help their organizations prosper by using their learning are the stars and help make the organization healthy for everyone.

As you read this story, think about whether you are a Buzz or a Buster. If you see more of yourself in Buster, accept the challenge to change your ways like Buster does to start making honey for your hive. The key is to *use* your learning to make a difference every day in your work.

Enjoy the story!

Once, in a land of fields and flowers, there lived two hives of bees. One hive was full of productive honeybees, and the other was full of their lazy neighbors. Both groups of bees were enlisted with the same task: pollination.

Flowers were scattered everywhere, and there was no shortage. The bees in the productive hive worked constantly to collect as much nectar as possible. Their only job was to bring pollen from flower to flower, ensuring the growth of the flowers and the production of nectar to make honey for the hive.

Everyone loves honey.

For one bee in particular, named Buzz, this job was exceptionally enjoyable. He found absolute delight in spending his days out in the sunlight, taking in the warmth and beauty of his surroundings. He'd quietly hum a tune as he worked, feeling as light as a feather.

The sunflowers were by far his favorites. He loved the bright yellow petals and the way they were always reaching up toward the sun. With his help, the sunflowers in his territory were flourishing. They were seven feet tall with golden petals and strong stalks that never wavered.

Transferring lots of pollen leads to sweet rewards.

Buzz had helped his sunflowers so much that they, in return, gave him enormous amounts of nectar to bring back to his hive, which was then used to make honey.

He was congratulated by his hive mates and rewarded with extra honey for his hard work. He became a star within his community and was honored with the position of chief pollinator.

Making honey makes the garden blossom.

One day, while attending to his duties out in the field, Buzz reached the border between his territory and the next field over. Buzz noticed that the flowers on the other side of the fence were wilting and losing their color.

He searched the flowers for any bees, hoping to find one working on the problem, but he found none. He lingered at the fence for a while, waiting for any sign of honeybees. He felt an urge to visit the neighboring hive to warn them of their dying flowers, but he knew that the bees would eventually realize the error of their ways. He reluctantly flew away from the fence and returned to his hive for the evening.

Having honey makes it hard to see opportunities to make more.

Meanwhile, in the neighboring hive, a honeybee named Buster sat in his room. His hive was quiet. His friends and family remained in their beds. They'd spent the whole day and many of the days before like this.

In fact, Buster couldn't remember the last time he'd gone outside or even seen anyone else leave the hive. He had heard tales from his parents of busy honeybees who used to work hard for the hive, and he and his friends had seen the fields of flowers those bees once buzzed in, but these days, this group of hive mates much preferred the comfort of their soft beds.

Don't laugh at what you don't understand.

Buster and his friends laughed at Buzz and his hive mates. Buster would stand at his window watching that whole hive flutter around the flowers. They'd fly from one to the other doing some sort of unfamiliar action, and then they'd move on to the next one. Buster and his friends found it strange that the other honeybees did this every day and that they seemed to enjoy this laborious activity.

It seemed like too much work to Buster and his friends. Why would anyone want to spend all day out in the hot sun? Buster and his friends would much rather stay inside where it was cool and they could sleep all day.

For his part, Buzz lingered at the fence every day. He couldn't understand why no one was fixing the flowers. By now, the flowers were almost dead. The wilted sunflowers on the ground almost made him cry. He couldn't stand to see such poor, neglected sunflowers.

And still, there were no bees anywhere to be seen! He told his friends about the situation, but they said there was nothing that could be done. Still, he refused to believe that all hope was lost.

Buzz waited at the fence every day, afraid to fly over it. It was unfamiliar territory, and he felt he had no place telling the other honeybees how to fix their flowers. At the same time, he couldn't stand to see dead flowers—especially sunflowers.

As much as it hurt Buzz to stand idly by, he still found himself doing nothing. But he'd return every day to watch over his newfound patch of flowers, and with all of his heart, he hoped that they would receive help soon.

If every bee transfers a little pollen each day, there'll be lots of honey for the hive.

In the other hive, Buster sighed, enjoying the silent passing of time as he finished another jar of honey. His life of no responsibilities had treated him well and left him with nothing but happiness. Searching for another honey jar, Buster soon realized that he'd finished the stock in his room. Pushing himself off of the ground, he moved to the stockroom to grab another jar.

As he opened the door, he found his hive mates in a panic. They were all searching, horribly confused about why, suddenly, all of their honey was gone.

It's hard to make honey by yourself.

"Did you guys run out of honey too?" Buster asked.

When they all nodded frantically, he rushed to find the hive's queen.

He shouted, "The honey's all gone!"

The queen shuddered awake and turned toward him, a frown on her face.

"Buster, the honey isn't gone. Don't joke around about things like that," she scolded.

"No, really, it's gone!" he exclaimed in reply.

The queen got up and flew toward the door.

"You and I both know that isn't true, Buster," she insisted.

Buster began to complain, but then he remembered that there was a bigger problem to deal with. He knew that once she saw that he was telling the truth, the queen would be able to figure out what to do.

He watched as the queen traveled to the stockroom and found a growing crowd of bees scrambling to find one full jar. When she realized that there was an actual need to panic, she began to join in the agitated buzzing about.

"All of the honey's gone!" one bee shouted.

"What should we do? We can't live without honey!" another exclaimed.

Buster began to feel the effects of the mass panic. His breath quickened, and he realized that he needed to get away from his family and friends. For once in his life, Buster moved through the main door.

The breeze abruptly hit him as he made his way outside. The sun shone brightly, making him squint as he flew. When Buster had room to breathe, he began to think about their dire situation.

When pollen is transferred, it makes hives and flowers strong.

How could they have let it get to this point? Long ago, all the honeybees had done their jobs and filled the hive with honey. But slowly, one honeybee after another had chosen not to apply their skill and knowledge of nectar gathering. The learning had not been passed down to the younger bees, and now they were all out of honey and all out of hope. Without honey, all of Buster's friends would die. At the thought of being all alone, Buster began to cry.

He slowly flew around their field, sobbing softly. How were they ever going to get more honey? They'd never learned how, and now they were out of luck.

As he passed over a clump of dead sunflowers, he heard a soft buzzing from nearby. As he moved closer to the fence, he noticed a small honeybee flying from flower to flower.

The flowers on that bee's side of the fence were completely healthy. The colors shone so vividly that they took Buster's breath away. He watched silently as the honeybee moved to one sunflower, dipping down into the center of it. When the honeybee came out of the flower, Buster noticed that his legs were covered in a yellow powder.

Buster watched as the honeybee moved to the next sunflower and did the exact same thing. Vaguely, Buster could remember his parents telling him about this work that honeybees used to do, but he had never tried it himself, so it all seemed new and strange.

Suddenly, the honeybee looked up. When it saw Buster, its eyes widened. "Are you from that hive over there?"

"Yes, I am. Are you a honeybee too?" Buster asked.

"Finally!" the bee shouted. "I've been waiting for you. My name is Buzz."

"I'm Buster. Why were you waiting for me?"

Training can help you make honey for your hive.

"Because your flowers are all dead! You need to pollinate them," Buzz announced.

"What's *pollinate*?" Buster asked.

"Are you kidding?" Buzz responded in shocked disbelief. "Pollination is how you keep your flowers alive and make honey."

"My hive and I need honey!" Buster said excitedly.

"If you pollinate your flowers, they'll give you nectar," Buzz explained. "You can use this nectar to make honey for your family and the rest of your hive."

"Can you teach me how to pollinate? My hive and I ran out of honey, and no one knows what to do."

"Why, of course I can!" Buzz replied. "I'll teach you, and then you can go and teach all of your friends. You'll have tons of honey in no time, I promise."

"Ugh, it's so hot! Why can't we go back inside?" Buster complained.

"Buster, you have to learn how to do this!" Buzz insisted. "You have to teach your hive."

"But it's so hot outside!" Buster exclaimed. "I have all this powdery stuff on me, and the flowers are still dead."

"It takes time. You have to be patient," Buzz said with a smile.

They'd been flying around for hours, Buzz teaching Buster every step of pollination. Buster quickly learned that it wasn't easy and that it would take some work.

*Making honey for your hive takes
some work, but it's worth it.*

Buzz quickly learned that Buster had never done any sort of laborious activity in his life. "It'll take some time to get used to, but it will all be worth it in the end," Buzz promised him.

"Whatever you say, Buzz," Buster groaned.

By the end of the day, Buzz had helped Buster pollinate all of the flowers on his side of the fence. It had taken longer than usual and had kept Buzz from doing his own work, but Buster was elated.

"How did you learn to do this?" Buster asked in wonder.

"I was taught by my parents. It's been a lifestyle for us honeybees for as long as I can remember, and it's kept us alive and strong," Buzz explained.

"I don't know if the rest of my hive will like working out in the sun, though," Buster said skeptically.

"You should at least go try. You need to show them that this will ensure their survival for the rest of their lives. It may take a little work, but the good things always do. If every single one of your friends pollinates a little each day, your hive will be full of honey in no time at all," Buzz promised.

"You're right, Buzz. Thank you for teaching me how to pollinate," Buster said with a smile.

"You're welcome. There won't be healthy flowers here for a while," Buzz further explained. "Pollination takes time, especially on flowers like yours. But soon enough, your sunflowers will look exactly like mine."

"I really hope so," Buster sighed. "I just have to convince everyone else to work for it."

Buster flew back to the entrance of the hive, his legs covered in pollen. He knocked on the door loudly, eager to tell the rest of his hive of his discovery.

Spreading pollen is easier than you think.

Buster's friends opened the door, looking sad and depressed.

"No one knows what to do about the honey," his friends sulked. "We used to know how to work to get more, but it was too hard. Now we'll starve."

"I think I know what to do," Buster said proudly, pushing past them.

"Is that why you've been gone so long?" he asked.

"Help me get everyone together, and I'll explain everything."

Making excuses not to pollinate kills the hive.

"Everyone, come see!" Buster shouted. "I have a surprise."

He waited patiently for the rest of his hive mates to make their way into the main room where he stood with a huge smile on his face. His friends started to buzz with anticipation as they noticed the pollen on his body.

"What is that?" one asked.

"Where did it come from?" another friend yelled from the back.

"I collected it," Buster exclaimed.

"Collected it? From where?" asked his friend.

"From the flowers outside," Buster replied.

"Flowers?" his friend said with a laugh. "Is that what the other bees are always doing?"

Buster nodded. "Buzz, one of the bees from the other side of the fence, showed me how to spread this pollen so we can get nectar from our flowers."

His friends began to laugh loudly.

"You didn't tell us you were friends with the other bees, Buster. You actually went out into the hot sun and worked like they do?" a hive mate asked in disbelief.

"Well, yes ... but it was worth it! Look!" he shouted, pointing to the pollen. "I can teach all of you how I did it, and then we'll have flowers with lots of nectar to make honey forever."

"If you think we are going to go work outside when we could be in here, you are very wrong," his friend replied.

"Please, just believe me," Buster begged. "I can help us. I promise. It's a process called pollination, and it's not really that hard."

"But we don't want to work," his friend spat.

"But it grows healthy flowers that give us nectar to make honey!" Buster insisted again. "Just give it a chance. We're all out. What do we have to lose?"

Pollen is worthless until it gets used.

His hive mates looked at one another, shrugging skeptically.

"All right, I guess," his friend sighed. "But we better get more honey fast."

Buster's hive mates were out in the hot sun only a moment or two before they started asking if they could go back inside.

"No, you can't!" Buster insisted, flying from flower to flower, searching for the perfect one to use to demonstrate the process of pollination.

When he finally found one, he asked the hive to gather around.

"Okay, this is pollen," he demonstrated, pointing to the small bit of yellow inside the center of the flower. "The reason all the flowers are dead is because they are running out of pollen. What we have to do is transfer the pollen from flower to flower and keep them alive," Buster instructed, just as Buzz had done for him.

"How is that going to give us honey?" one bee shouted.

"Well, once all of the flowers are healthy again, they'll give us nectar in return, which we can use to make honey," Buster said in excitement.

"That seems like a lot of work," one of the bees said with boredom. "Look at how many flowers there are!"

"But if we work together, we can make enough honey for all of us. And quickly, too!" Buster said reassuringly, trying to convince his hive mates.

"But won't we just run out again?" his friend asked.

"Not if we keep working and collect nectar from the flowers," Buster replied. "It'll take constant work, and we'll have to assign teams and organize shifts, but we can do it!" He smiled, confident in his friends.

"Are you sure?" they asked.

"Yes." He grinned. "Now come help me."

One honeybee broke from the group, joining Buster at the flower. Buster showed the bee how to pick up pollen with its legs and transfer it to the next flower. Soon enough, all the bees were lining up to take their turn.

"Hey, ummm ... Buster?" one of his friends asked. "Thanks for your help. We couldn't have figured this out without you." Buster's friend smiled.

Buster felt his heart swell with pride, knowing that not only had he made a new friend in Buzz, but he'd done something good that would help his hive carry on forever.

All the while, Buzz watched from the window of his honeybee hive. A smile graced his face as he noticed the honeybees working in the field. He watched joyfully as they made their way to each flower. He recognized Buster at the front and watched as Buster demonstrated how to pollinate the flowers.

All hives need a leader to teach others how to make honey.

With a little work, Buster's hive would be filled with honey in no time. All they needed was to change their ways, learn new skills, and put them to use.

The End

Lessons about Learning Transfer

1. Everyone loves honey.
2. Transferring lots of pollen leads to sweet rewards.
3. Making honey makes the garden blossom.
4. Having honey makes it hard to see opportunities to make more.
5. Don't laugh at what you don't understand.
6. If every bee transfers a little pollen each day, there'll be lots of honey for the hive.
7. It's hard to make honey by yourself.
8. When pollen is transferred, it makes hives and flowers strong.
9. Training can help you make honey for your hive.
10. Making honey for your hive takes a some work, but it's worth it.
11. Spreading pollen is easier than you think.
12. Making excuses not to pollinate kills the hive.
13. Pollen is worthless until it gets used.
14. All hives need a leader to teach others how to make honey.

Conclusion

Organizations are like Buzz's and Buster's beehives. They depend on employees like Buzz and Buster to work hard every day to make them successful. Imagine for a minute what would happen to your organization if it was filled with Buster-type bees who refused to use their learning. What would the result be?

You know the answer: failure. Organizations depend on their employees to learn every day. But learning alone is not enough. In organizational life, having employees who simply know more "stuff" doesn't help. Learners must take their learning and *apply* it to their jobs in order for the organization to prosper.

This fable illustrates the transfer process as pollen is carried from flower to flower, making them strong and healthy. The result is lots of sweet nectar, which the bees turn into honey. Just like the bees, if we carry our learning from the classroom to our jobs, the result will be good outcomes for everyone. Refuse to do it, and in time the flowers die, just like organizations do.

Thus, learning transfer is not just another HR issue that can be ignored. Learning that is *used* is the lifeblood of every organization. Think for a moment about how much learning gets used in your organization. What if that amount doubled? What would the impact be?

In most organizations, the impact would be incredible. The amount of performance change would be amazing. Now, imagine that your employer is much more successful. How would that impact you? For most employees, the personal impact would also be amazing.

Learning transfer is everyone's responsibility, and fixing it will benefit everyone. Like Buster, you can be a hero for significantly increasing how much you apply what you learn on your job.

Learning is the nectar of organizational success. But just like the honeybee, you have to collect it *and* use it in the hive to get the sweet rewards.

Open Book Editions
A Berrett-Koehler Partner

Open Book Editions is a joint venture between Berrett-Koehler Publishers and Author Solutions, the market leader in self-publishing. There are many more aspiring authors who share Berrett-Koehler's mission than we can sustainably publish. To serve these authors, Open Book Editions offers a comprehensive self-publishing opportunity.

A Shared Mission

Open Book Editions welcomes authors who share the Berrett-Koehler mission—Creating a World That Works for All. We believe that to truly create a better world, action is needed at all levels—individual, organizational, and societal. At the individual level, our publications help people align their lives with their values and with their aspirations for a better world. At the organizational level, we promote progressive leadership and management practices, socially responsible approaches to business, and humane and effective organizations. At the societal level, we publish content that advances social and economic justice, shared prosperity, sustainability, and new solutions to national and global issues.

Open Book Editions represents a new way to further the BK mission and expand our community. We look forward to helping more authors challenge conventional thinking, introduce new ideas, and foster positive change.

For more information, see the Open Book Editions website: http://www.iuniverse.com/Packages/OpenBookEditions.aspx

Join the BK Community! See exclusive author videos, join discussion groups, find out about upcoming events, read author blogs, and much more! http://bkcommunity.com/

www.ingramcontent.com/pod-product-compliance
Lightning Source LLC
Chambersburg PA
CBHW071640170526
45166CB00003B/1374